Few pieces of mine

mine

Part-1

(A poetry collection)

Contents

<u>Part-2</u>

Poem 11 - I'm the joy

Poem 12 - I pulled a thread from the yarn of thoughts

Poem 13 - I'm a freak

Poem 14 - What a massacre!

Poem 15 - On March 17th

Poem 16 - Today I covet

Poem 17 - Further away I go

Poem 18 - A banana shot me!

Poem 19 - Let's write something

Poem 20 - I felt his absence

<u>Acknowledgments</u>

To my readers, I'd like to talk about what this book or this poetry collection is about. It's not hard to describe it, it is just a poetry collection with an artsy name 'few pieces of mine' but I chose this name for this poetry collection because these poems in some way are a piece of me, they're my own imaginations and as any other writer, I too want to share my thoughts with an audience or a reader not to only make money but to see what other people think of it, do they like it? If yes, then what did they liked about it? Do they hate it? If they do then how do I improve myself? that's what I'm trying to do, I want to share my art with others to see whether they like it or not because if people didn't like the stuff I'm writing then who would even buy it? Not many people, so I just hope that when you read it, there would be something that you'd like about these poems.

To my family, who supported me, to my brother, my mother and specifically to my father who has faith in me that one day I'd do great things in the future and it's this faith that keeps me going, he's been my guide since the day I born. I'm so grateful for my family and the support they gave me.

To my cousin brothers, who read my poems and gave me a review of everything I wrote up until now, I shared with them my poems and asked them if they like it and they did like it which gave me more confidence.

To my friend, Utsav Acharya whom I worked with in a school project and he helped me a lot with writing since then and he still reviews my work whenever he has time, he always gives me a constructive review of everything I write and I make corrections if there are any to make.

To my teachers, who taught me a thing or two about life and it's only because of them that I am able to perceive the world the way I do.

And at last I want to thank you, my readers for reading these poems written by a nobody, I am one of you, I'm also a boy with a lot of big dreams and I thank you readers as now you've become a part of my world, thank you once again for being the part of this journey.

1- What am I?

What am I?
A man, a monster,
Why my hands never shake?
Why am I so cold blooded?

I didn't flinch,
When I first killed,
What am I?
A nightmare, who haunted innocents,
Who butchered women and children,

Why did I stopped showing every emotion we
humans have,
Pain, empathy and conscience,
I lost them all,
Long ago,

What am I?
Why don't I hate myself the way I should?
Why do I enjoy myself so much?

What happened to that squeamish son-of-a-bitch,
Why is he gone?
I wanted to feel something,
But I can't,
And now I ask myself,
what am I?
What've I become?
A monster?
A nightmare?

2-I saw a sketch of you, naked !

I saw a sketch of you, naked,

Just standing there,

I saw a sketch of you in my dreams,

Never thought of you as a person,

A projection of my lust, an object perhaps,

I saw you naked,

It felt real, your breasts, your hairs, they felt real,

It was spellbinding,

I saw you dancing,

You'd no worries,

It was my dream,

And you were happy in it,

Whoever who were,
 I saw a sketch of you,
You were there,
I stared at you,
I drooled over you,
I saw a sketch of you,
Naked!

3-Before I fly

Before I fly,

I was on the ground,

Staring at the stars,

A thought came to me,

Where should I go?

I am afraid of flying,

What if I died?

It'd be nauseating, won't it?

But why these questions,

Would I ever fly?

I don't have wings,

Do I need them?

I was calm,

Sitting on a bench,

I was scared of letting it go,

What if people saw me flying?
They'd desire what I've done,
They'll too chase the dreams I always had,
A dream, to fly without no worries,
They'll chase me,

But I won't move,
I don't want to,
I am too scared of falling,
I don't want to be a joke,

I should close my eyes,
 And think about where should I go,
I've been afraid of flying my whole life,
Now I'll just spread my hands,
And I'll just go wherever the wind shall take me,
I don't care if I die or if people mock me,
I will either be a clown or a hero,

I had a long life,

And I'm happy with it,

Before I fly,

I saw a man who jumped and tried to fly but failed,

Maybe I'd fall too,

Whatever happens,

I don't care anymore,

I hope,

I hope it won't matter if I fail,

And the only thing that matters is at least

I tried to fly.

4- <u>Nobody knows the man I once wanted to be</u>

Nobody knows the man I once wanted to be,

Just searching for a McGuffin which I never desired,

Why should they know that man?

He was lost,

a stranger to himself,

Just drifting away from reality,

Living a dream of being a perfect man,

A man he was taught to be by his father,

Maybe I could've become that man,

But it remains a dream,

People need that man,

To project their own dreams and unfulfilled desires,

My father was one of them,

But he never forced me to be that man,

Maybe he realised I can't be that man,

I was restless back then,

I was trying but nobody knows that,

What has changed in me?

I am restless now,

I never got to know about that McGuffin,

And now I never will,

Was it worth looking for?

What if I'd become the man I once wanted to be?

No one knows the man I once wanted to be,

And now no one will,

That man is long gone,

With no ambition in my life,

I stare at the void which once was filled with something.

5- <u>It was all in vain!</u>

It was all in vain!

This relationship we built together,

This home we built together,

It was all in vain!

' what've we done to each other?'

' where do we stand now?'

I wake up,

I ask these questions,

'where have I gone wrong?'

A thought relentlessly torturing me,

I eloped with you,

My parents asleep,

I ran for you,

The moment I met you,

I knew you were the one,

That night I ran for you,

I was being rebellious,

I was being foolish,

But the adrenaline didn't stopped me from going on,

Nor did my parents,

' What do we do now?'

'How are we supposed to live now?'

'Where are we supposed to live now?'

'What's next?'

'Is this our life now?'

I never even thought about these questions,

I built this house together with you,

we named it hope,

It had a kitchen,

A bed,

And a living room,

We breathed life into these lifeless woods,

We worked together everyday,

You loved me,

And I loved you,

I loved this little house we called 'HOPE',

I loved every moment I spent with you in that house,

I had a big smile on my face everyday,

But the foundation of our house started to crumble,

I got pregnant,

I was happy,

But he wasn't,

He was there,

But, not with me,

A marriage that stood strong for two years,

Started to crumble,

It fell apart when the truth was revealed,

He was a monster,

He'd beat my baby,

Yell at her,

One night, I eloped with my daughter,

He was asleep,

And she was crying,

I left him,
I ran away,
And didn't stop,
Here I'm today,
Holding my dearest,
Just thinking,
'it was all in vain!
'It was a mistake!'

6- <u>What if?</u>

What if I was there with you,

When you where growing up,

When you went to your prom night with you,

When you lost your hand,

When you lost your unborn baby,

What if?

I was there when you were lying on the hospital bed,

Thinking about committing suicide,

When you were silently crying under those

Soothing shadows of the oak,

What if?

I was there when you slept with that man,

Who broke you,

Made you feel empty,

Made you destroyed your beautiful body for him,

What if?

I was there when you got shot,

When you were jumping out of joy after graduating,

And when you earned your first salary,

What if I was there with you?

What would've I done?

Maybe I would've loved you the way that man couldn't,

Maybe I would've protected you from that monster,

Maybe I would've hugged you when you were feeling miserable,

Maybe I would've consoled you in the hospital,

But what if I'd done nothing,

And left you just like everyone else.

7- <u>I ran</u>

I ran,

I tried,

I reached from afar,

I started walking on a plain,

And now I've reached on a plateau,

But I couldn't move anymore,

I am tired,

I ran in the same direction for years,

I ran when I should've walked,

And now I don't know where to go,

I should've been there for you,

You were helpless,

Just longing for someone you love,

But I didn't show up,

I'm not weak,

I'm not a coward,

But sometimes I just run away,

I run away from responsibilities,

I run away from those who I love,

Fearing that maybe I'd lose them,

I ran,

I tried,

What could've I done anyways?

Am I a coward?

I ran that day when you were in pain,

I couldn't even look at you,

I just ran,

8- <u>I thought you were a fly</u>

I thought you were a fly,

You'd always wonder around beautiful flowers,

You always admired the beauty of them,

I don't know if I'm a flower to be desired,

Or to be washed away a splash of water,

Maybe one day you'd sit on this flower

I sow years ago,

I could just take you in my hands and put you on it,

You won't even be able to resist,

I wouldn't let you,

But I want you to wander around with freedom,

As that's when you're most beautiful,

This flower of mine will blossom one day,

But you won't be there,

It'd be lonely, stranded in the sea of beauty,

And just like that it'd be gone forever,

Even if someone like you say on it,

It'd be gone forever someday,

What remains is the essence of it,

The beauty it once was,

Just like you,

One day you'd be gone too,

But you'd always be a beautiful fly to me,

And to the flowers you sat on,

I thought you were a fly,

I let you go,

Even if you'd stung me,

I'd let you go,

Because you were beautiful,

I beauty I've always admired from afar.

9-IT WON'T MATTER

Should I scream?

Should I cry?

What should I do?

It won't matter in the end,

I don't want dreams, ambitions,

I don't have the hunger,

I never had to beg for it,

But where would I end up?

It won't matter,

I think about the sea,

I want to be like that,

I want to keep going,

Sometimes faster,

Sometimes slower,

And sometimes I want to be still,

I just want to keep going

Without a fix destination,

it doesn't matter where I'll end up,

It won't matter,

Maybe it'll matter to someone else,

Maybe! But, it doesn't to me,

Maybe because I'm afraid,

I'm afraid that I'll fail,

And people would laugh at me,

I don't want to care,

Maybe then death won't be harsh for me,

As then I'd have nothing to lose,

I'd be happy then,

It won't matter if I disappeared in the crowd,

It won't matter if I lived a mediocre life,

Because one day everything'll be gone,

And I'll just feel empty anyways,

You call me a coward,

Maybe I'm,

But in the end,

When I'd be dying,

It won't matter.

10- <u>A meaning lost in interpretation</u>

A meaning lost in interpretation,

Is like a thousand deaths for me,

I made something beautiful, simple and ingenious,

Thought about it for days and nights,

Why must you destroy it?

'I was tired & I died'

That's my story,

It's a simple truth,

Why can't you accept that?

'I saw a tree & slept in it's shadow',

Why don't you accept that,

Why it has to be so fucking complicated?

You don't see the truth,

You don't see a story,

You saw a mirror,

In that mirror you projected,

You projected your stupidity onto it,

'I was stabbed in the back by a coward',

Why can't you understand that?

Admit you're a fool,

And a fool you'd always be,

A meaning lost in interpretation,

A body bathing in pain and sorrow,

Pain that you didn't want what's it created,

A sorrow that this is not going to change,

I cried and I laughed,

I was in pain,

And you gave it to me,

You weren't there,

You never experienced it,

You just saw it,

Interpret it, but let it be simple,

Don't make it hard for me to recognise it,

A meaning lost in interpretation,

And just a shadow left,

A shadow of what I really intended,

A story died.